© 2025 Scott L. Gordon

All rights reserved. No part of this publication may be reproduced, stored, or transmitted by any means—electronic, mechanical, photocopying, recording, or otherwise—without written permission from the author

First Edition – 2025
Printed in the United States of America

Dedication

To everyone who ever felt forgotten,
overlooked, or counted out—
May this story remind you:
God still writes with broken pens.

About the Author

Scott L. Gordon is a visionary leader, pastor, real estate developer, and author who has spent his life transforming pain into purpose. With over two decades of experience in ministry and economic development, he has built and remodeled and transformed many homes, pastored faithfully, and mentored leaders across the globe. His passion is to restore broken places and broken people with faith, wisdom, and integrity. Scott's books and teachings inspire others to live boldly, believe fiercely, and build with legacy in mind.

Introduction

Your thoughts are the steering wheel of your life. Where your mind goes, your life will follow. This book was birthed from years of personal battles, leadership moments, and divine revelation that taught me the truth—if you can change your mind, you can change everything. These chapters are not theory—they're life-tested principles, born in prayer, pain, and persistence. As you read, don't just take notes. Make decisions. Your future is too important to be held hostage by an old mindset. It's time to change how you think—and change your life.

PART: 1

Change Your Thinking Change Your World

By Scott Gordon

Chapter 1: The Mind Is the Battlefield

From the book: Change Your Mind, Change Your Life by Scott Gordon

---

I'll never forget the day I sat in my office, worn out—not from preaching, not from hospital visits, not even from funerals—but from frustration. The kind that seeps into your bones when you've poured everything you have into people, only to see them still stuck in the same place. Not because God didn't move. Not because the Word wasn't preached. But because their mindset never changed.

Ministry will teach you real quick that deliverance doesn't always look like a shout. Sometimes it's a decision. And the truth is, I've watched people cry in the altar and walk right back into the same mental trap that's been stealing their peace for years. That's what breaks a pastor's heart.

Early in my pastorate at Calvary, I thought passion alone could fix people. That if I just prayed harder, preached bolder, and loved deeper, the chains would fall. And sometimes they did. But what I began to see over the years was a pattern—people who were faithful in church, but defeated in life. They had the form, but not the freedom. They were shouting "Amen!" on Sunday and still drowning in doubt on Monday.

The problem wasn't the enemy outside. It was the enemy inside.

God had to show me: until their mind is renewed, their life won't change.

Romans 12:2 became more than a memory verse—it became my mission. "Be not conformed to this world, but be ye transformed by the renewing of your mind..." I realized I wasn't just called to help people get saved. I was called to help them think differently. To pull down strongholds—not just of sin, but of stinking thinking.

Chapter 1: The Mind Is the Battlefield

I've sat across from young men who had talent, calling, and opportunity—but who were stuck because they couldn't believe they were more than what they came from. I've watched women, strong in the Spirit, sabotaged by a mindset shaped by rejection and fear. And I've seen whole families pass down not just habits, but mindsets—poverty, bitterness, insecurity—all because nobody taught them how to renew their mind

That's why I'm writing this book. Not just to inspire, but to impart. Because I've learned that if you can change your thinking, you can change everything.

You're not in bondage to your past. You're not stuck in cycles because of curses. Many times, you're just trapped in a thought pattern that doesn't line up with God's Word.

And until you change your mind, your life won't follow.

In this chapter—and in the pages to come—I'm inviting you to do the hard work of mind renewal. To dig into the Word like never before. To replace lies with truth. And to step into the freedom Jesus already paid for.

PART 1: Change Your Thinking Change Your World

Because the battlefield isn't just in the world. It's not just in your job, your finances, or your relationships.

It's in your mind.

Chapter 2: The Prison of the Old Mindset

From the book: Change Your Mind, Change Your Life by Scott Gordon

---

I've come to learn something that took years of ministry to truly understand: people can walk out of Egypt and still carry Egypt in their mind.

You can come to the altar, cry real tears, get up, and still go home mentally chained to a place God already brought you out of. Freedom isn't just about physical deliverance. It's about mental transformation.

When the children of Israel left Egypt, they left behind bricks, whips, and pharaohs. But they carried something with them that wouldn't die easy—the mindset of slavery. And it showed every time they were tested. Instead

PART 1: Change Your Thinking Change Your World

of trusting God, they complained. Instead of moving forward, they wanted to go back. They were free, but not yet free.

That's the danger of old mindsets. They convince you that your past was safer than your potential.

I remember counseling a man who had just gotten out of prison. He came to church faithfully, got a job, started trying to rebuild his life. But every time pressure came—every time life got too real—he'd retreat into survival mode. Not criminal activity, but emotional shutdown. He still thought like an inmate. Distrustful. Defensive. Always waiting for something bad to happen. One day he told me, "Pastor, I don't know how to think free. I know how to do time, but I don't know how to live."

That hit me deep. Because I realized—so many of us are just like him. We're not behind bars, but we're still in prison. Mental prisons. Emotional prisons. Relational prisons. We've been set free by Jesus, but we've never been taught how to think like we're free.

Chapter 2: The Prison of the Old Mindset

It's why so many believers get saved but stay stuck. They know church, but they don't know change. They quote scriptures but still fight with fear. They pray for a new season but keep showing up with the same mindset.

Deliverance got them out. But transformation never got in.

And I get it. Mindsets are tricky. They don't always show up loud. Sometimes they're quiet assumptions you've carried your whole life: "I'm not enough." "Nothing ever works for me." "I guess I'm just not meant to be happy." These aren't just thoughts—they're beliefs. And beliefs shape behavior.

Let me tell you—God can bless you with a new opportunity, but if your mindset hasn't changed, you'll sabotage it. You'll shrink back. You'll push people away. You'll talk yourself out of what God already said yes to.

One of the hardest things I've had to do in ministry is confront people I love about the way they think. Because we don't just need encouragement—we need alignment.

PART 1: Change Your Thinking Change Your World

Encouragement says, "You can make it." Alignment says, "But you've got to think differently if you want to."

That's why Romans 12:2 is so powerful. "Be transformed by the renewing of your mind." Not by shouting, not by church attendance, not even by miracles—but by renewal. That word in the Greek implies renovation. Tearing down old thought patterns. Replacing what's broken. Installing what's true.

I've watched people pray for a husband or wife, but still think like someone unworthy of love. So even when God sends the right person, their insecurity drives them to ruin the relationship. That's the prison of the old mindset.

I've seen entrepreneurs try to launch businesses but quit after the first setback—not because they lacked potential, but because deep down they didn't believe success was possible for "someone like me." That's the voice of Egypt whispering in a Promised Land moment.

But here's the good news: you don't have to stay stuck. You don't have to carry the old you into the new place

Chapter 2: The Prison of the Old Mindset

God is taking you.

God gave us the key. And it starts with the Word. With replacing every lie you've believed with the truth of what God says about you. You are not your past. You are not your pain. You are not your parents' mistakes. You are not what they did to you.

You are free. And it's time your mind caught up with your spirit.

This chapter is your turning point. If you're ready to stop circling the same mental wilderness, this is your moment to step forward. Not just with your feet, but with your faith. Not just into a new place—but into a new mindset.

Because real freedom doesn't come when the chains fall off. Real freedom comes when you stop reaching back to pick them up.

Change your mind. Leave the prison. And walk in the promise.

Chapter 3: Faith Over Focus

From the book: Change Your Mind, Change Your Life by Scott Gordon

---

I remember sitting across the table from a young man who had just lost everything. His business had failed, his marriage was hanging on by a thread, and he said these words to me I'll never forget: "Pastor, I can't see God in this."

And I told him what I've had to tell myself more times than I can count: "That doesn't mean He's not there. It means your focus is off."

Because focus determines direction. And whatever has your focus will shape your future.

That young man wasn't faithless—he was distracted. And distraction is one of the enemy's most effective tools. If

PART 1: Change Your Thinking Change Your World

the devil can't destroy you, he'll distract you. He'll flood your mind with noise, fear, and confusion until you stop looking at the promise and start staring at the problem.

Peter knows what that feels like.

In Matthew 14, Peter did something no other human being outside of Jesus ever did—he walked on water. And it wasn't magic. It wasn't a trick. It was a moment of pure faith. Jesus simply said, "Come," and Peter stepped out of the boat.

But the Bible says that *when he saw the wind and waves, he became afraid and began to sink*.

What happened? His focus shifted.

As long as his eyes were on Jesus, he was doing the impossible. But the moment his attention turned to the storm, he lost his footing. Not because the power left him—but because the fear overtook him.

Focus will either feed your faith or starve it.
It's up to you.

Chapter 3: Faith Over Focus

I've learned in ministry—and in my own life—that most people don't need a new word from God. They need to refocus on what He already said. God hasn't changed His mind, but many times we've changed our focus.

You can't walk in power while staring at problems. You can't live in purpose while focusing on pain. And you'll never win the battle in your mind if your eyes are constantly on what's wrong instead of Who's right there with you.

Years ago, I was going through a season where everything felt like it was falling apart. The church was under pressure, the real estate business was struggling, and I was carrying more than I could even explain. I wasn't sleeping. I wasn't eating right. I was drained spiritually.

I remember one night, sitting in my car outside the church parking lot just staring into the dark, asking God, "Where are You in all of this?"

And the Holy Spirit gently reminded me: *You're looking at the storm, but I never told you to stop walking.*

PART 1: Change Your Thinking Change Your World

I had allowed the winds around me to pull my gaze away from the One who called me in the first place.

And that's the lesson. Faith doesn't deny the storm. It just doesn't bow to it. Faith doesn't ignore the waves—it walks above them.

But only if your focus stays in the right place.

Paul said in Philippians 4:8, "Think on these things..." Not fear, not failure, not frustration. Things that are true, noble, just, pure, lovely, and of good report. Why? Because what you focus on determines your mental diet. And your mental diet shapes your emotional health, your decisions, and your future.

If all you feed on is bad news, gossip, trauma, and negativity, don't be surprised when your faith feels weak. Your faith is starving because your focus is toxic.

But if you start feeding on the Word... if you start meditating on God's promises... if you start speaking life instead of death—everything changes.

Chapter 3: Faith Over Focus

I've had to train my mind to shift. Not to ignore reality, but to elevate my perspective. When fear whispers, "It's over," faith shouts back, "It's not finished!" When doubt says, "You'll never make it," the Word says, "I can do all things through Christ."

Your thoughts are seeds. And your focus is the water. What are you watering?

You can't expect faith to grow when all you water is fear.

In this chapter, I want you to get honest with yourself. Where has your focus been? On the waves? On the wind? Or on the One who called you to walk above it all?

Peter didn't fail because of the storm. He failed because of his focus.

But don't miss the grace in the story—Jesus reached out and caught him. And He'll catch you too.

Even when you lose focus, He doesn't lose you.

PART 1: Change Your Thinking Change Your World

Let this be the moment you shift. The storm might still be raging. The waves might still be rising. But if your eyes are on Jesus, you'll walk on what was meant to drown you.

Because your faith will rise to meet your focus.

Change your focus. Strengthen your faith. Walk in your calling.

Chapter 4: Rewire Your Mind with the Word

From the book: Change Your Mind, Change Your Life by Scott Gordon

---

If you don't like what your life is producing, you have to check what your mind is planting.

I used to think the answer to a mental battle was just "pray about it." And don't get me wrong—prayer is powerful. But there were times when I was praying and still struggling. Crying out to God, yet waking up with the same fear, the same anxiety, the same weight pressing on my chest.

PART 1: Change Your Thinking Change Your World

Until God showed me something simple but life-changing: "You're rebuking the thought, but you're not replacing it."

You can't just cast down negative thinking—you have to build up godly thinking in its place. You have to rewire your mind with the Word.

Joshua 1:8 became my manual for mental breakthrough: "This Book of the Law shall not depart from your mouth, but you shall meditate on it day and night..."

That verse doesn't say "visit the Word occasionally." It says *meditate.* That's where the rewiring happens.

When you meditate on something, you chew on it, speak it, mutter it under your breath. You let it shape your thoughts until it becomes part of your internal wiring. And that's what many people miss. They hear the Word, but they don't let it *live* in them.

There was a time in my life when I felt surrounded by failure. Every area of my life felt under attack. Ministry,

Chapter 4: Rewire Your Mind with the Word

finances, even my confidence. I was leading people while silently questioning if I was even hearing God anymore.

That's when I had to go back to the basics. I took out a journal and started writing down every lie I was battling—and next to each one, I wrote a scripture to replace it.

"I'm not enough." → *Philippians 4:13 – I can do all things through Christ who strengthens me.*

"This will never get better." → *Romans 8:28 – All things work together for good...*

"I'm going to lose everything." → *Psalm 37:25 – I've never seen the righteous forsaken...*

Every morning, before I faced people, pressure, or problems—I faced those declarations.

At first it felt like I was faking it. But I wasn't faking—I was *training*. And slowly, my mind started to change. Not because of willpower, but because of Word power.

PART 1: Change Your Thinking Change Your World

You have to understand, your brain builds pathways. Every time you repeat a thought, it deepens that mental groove. That's why fear becomes automatic. Doubt becomes second nature. But the Word of God is powerful enough to carve out a new path. A new mental highway of truth.

The more you speak it, the more you believe it. The more you believe it, the more you live it.

I started preaching this to my congregation—not just sermons, but strategies. I'd challenge people: "Don't just hear this message. Go home and make a confession list. Find scriptures that fight your strongest thoughts."

Some did it and saw breakthrough. Others didn't—and stayed stuck. Not because they weren't spiritual, but because they didn't follow the strategy.

That's what makes Joshua so powerful. Before he led Israel into battle, God didn't tell him to sharpen his sword. He told him to sharpen his *mind*. "Meditate on this day and night… then you will make your way prosperous and have good success."

Chapter 4: Rewire Your Mind with the Word

You want success? You want peace? You want a transformed life? You need a transformed mind.

Let me say this clearly: You cannot win a spiritual war with a carnal thought life.

You've got to soak your mind in the truth. Declare it out loud. Memorize it. Let it become so embedded in you that when fear comes, the Word rises first.

I know this works. I've lived it. I've watched the Word become my anchor in seasons when everything was shaking.

When my heart was broken, it was the Word that held me. When my mind was attacked, it was the Word that covered me. When I couldn't trust what I felt, I stood on what I *knew*—and that was the Word of God.

And now I tell every person I lead: don't just quote a scripture once. Make it your confession until it becomes your reality.

PART 1: Change Your Thinking Change Your World

You have the power to rewire your mind. Not with motivational quotes. Not with mantras. But with the living, breathing Word of the Almighty God.

Start today. Write the lie. Find the truth. Speak it. Declare it. And watch your mind align with the power of heaven.

Because your next level of freedom is waiting on the other side of your obedience.

Rewire your thoughts. Reset your faith. And renew your life.

Chapter 5: Talking Back to Your Thoughts

From the book: Change Your Mind, Change Your Life by Scott Gordon

---

I've had to learn something as a pastor, a man, and a believer: just because a thought enters your mind doesn't mean you have to agree with it.

You don't have to believe every voice in your head. You don't have to cosign every fear. You don't have to accept every whisper of doubt that tries to tell you you're not enough.

You can talk back.

David showed us how.

PART 1: Change Your Thinking Change Your World

In Psalm 42:5, he says, "Why, my soul, are you downcast? Why so disturbed within me? Put your hope in God…" That wasn't David talking to God. That was David talking to *himself.*

He was in the middle of emotional turmoil—surrounded by enemies, feeling forgotten, overwhelmed by sorrow—and yet, instead of letting those emotions rule him, he turned inward and had a conversation with his soul.

Why? Because sometimes, your soul needs a reminder. Your emotions need a realignment. Your mind needs a reset.

And no one can do that for you. You have to do it for yourself.

I'll be honest—there have been days where I didn't feel like preaching, leading, or even getting out of bed. Days where my own thoughts said, "You're done." "You blew it." "Nobody's listening." "This is too much."

Chapter 5: Talking Back to Your Thoughts

And I had to learn to do what David did. I had to speak *truth* louder than the lies. I had to open my mouth and declare the Word of God, even when I didn't feel like it.

Because if you stay silent, the thoughts will take over.

You can't fight negative thoughts with more thoughts. You fight them with words. Spoken, faith-filled, Bible-backed *words.*

Think about Jesus in the wilderness. When the enemy tempted Him, He didn't think about scriptures—He *spoke* them. "It is written…" was His weapon.

And if Jesus had to talk back, what makes us think we don't?

One of the greatest tactics of the enemy is internal accusation. He'll use your own mind to condemn you. To tell you you're unworthy, too far gone, disqualified. And if you're not careful, you'll come into agreement with a lie that doesn't even belong to you.

But you have the authority to respond. To say, "No—that's not who I am." "No—I will not fear." "No—I won't accept that as truth."

Years ago, during a very dark season, I found myself battling depression that didn't come from circumstances—it came from internal weight. From years of pouring out without filling back up. From people leaving the church I gave my life to. From feeling like I had to always be strong even when I was silently struggling.

One night, I was driving home alone, and I felt it come over me like a wave: a lie that said, "You're not needed. You've failed. Just quit."

I pulled over. Turned the engine off. Sat there in silence.

Then I remembered David. And I said out loud, "Why are you downcast, Scott? Hope in God. You've seen Him make a way before. You've seen Him restore what was lost. Get your mind back in alignment."

It wasn't instant. But it was effective.

Chapter 5: Talking Back to Your Thoughts

Because when you talk back with truth, your thoughts have to bow.

I started doing this regularly. Not just in crisis moments, but as a habit. I'd speak into my own mornings before the day could speak into me.

"No matter what comes today, I am more than a conqueror."

"This situation is temporary, but God's Word is eternal."
"I am loved. I am called. I am covered."

I began to teach this to my leaders, too. "Don't just read the Word—*declare* it. Don't just think truth—*speak* it."

And it started transforming people. One sister in our church battled anxiety for years. I challenged her to write down five scriptures and declare them every morning for 30 days. She came back with tears in her eyes: "Pastor, I've had more peace this month than I've had in years."

This works. But you have to *do* it.

David didn't wait for someone else to encourage him. He encouraged *himself* in the Lord.

And you can do the same.

Here's how you start:

    1. Identify the recurring negative thought. Name it. Don't deny it.
    2. Find a scripture that speaks directly against it.
    3. Speak that scripture out loud—daily, repeatedly, until it becomes your reflex.

Because talking back isn't weakness—it's warfare.

You're not crazy for hearing voices. We all do. The question is: what voice are you agreeing with?

Silence the voice of the accuser with the voice of the Advocate—Jesus, the Word made flesh.

When fear speaks, speak louder. When doubt rises, lift up truth. When shame creeps in, declare grace.

Chapter 5: Talking Back to Your Thoughts

You don't have to live tormented in your own head. You have the right—and the responsibility—to fight back.

Talk back to your thoughts. And take back your peace.

Chapter 6: From Complaint to Confession

From the book: Change Your Mind, Change Your Life by Scott Gordon

---

I used to think I was just "venting." Just being real. Just expressing what I felt.

But then the Holy Spirit pulled me aside—right in the middle of a prayer—and said, "That's not venting, that's complaining. And it's keeping you stuck."

It hit me hard.

Because I was in a season where I couldn't figure out why things weren't moving. I was doing the work, showing up, preaching the Word—but personally, emotionally, and mentally, I was stalled. Until God showed me: it

PART 1: Change Your Thinking Change Your World

wasn't my hands that needed adjusting. It was my mouth. You can't speak defeat and expect to walk in victory.

There's power in your words. Proverbs 18:21 says it plainly: *"Death and life are in the power of the tongue."* Not just in what others say about you—but in what *you* say about yourself.

I began to look back on my conversations. I realized how often I complained—not just about problems, but about people, about progress, even about my own purpose.

And the problem with complaining is that it reinforces what's *wrong* instead of releasing what's *possible.*

Israel did this in the wilderness. God had just delivered them from Egypt—plagues, miracles, Red Sea-splitting, the whole deal. And yet, the moment they got uncomfortable, they started murmuring.

"We should've stayed in Egypt." "At least we had food back there." "Why did Moses bring us out here to die?"

Chapter 6: From Complaint to Confession

What happened? Their words locked them out of their promise.

A journey that should've taken days stretched into forty years. Not because of giants, but because of grumbling.

Let that sink in.

Their mouths delayed their movement.

And we do the same. Every time we speak fear instead of faith… every time we declare doubt instead of destiny… every time we replay the problem instead of declaring the promise—we participate in our own paralysis.

But here's the shift: confession.

I'm not talking about confessing sin. I'm talking about *confessing truth.* About opening your mouth and speaking the Word of God *on purpose.*

Philippians 4:8 says, "Whatsoever things are true, honest, just, pure, lovely, of good report… think on these things." But don't stop at thinking—*speak* those things.

PART 1: Change Your Thinking Change Your World

Your mouth steers your mindset.

If you keep saying, "I'm tired… I'm broke… I'm stressed… I'm overwhelmed…"—you're building a mental framework that agrees with that reality.

But if you start saying, "I am strong in the Lord… I am blessed and not cursed… I have peace that surpasses understanding… I'm the head and not the tail…"—your brain starts building a new framework. One that agrees with heaven.

Years ago, I had a lady in our church who came to me frustrated. She said, "Pastor, I just feel like nothing is changing. My prayers aren't working. My kids aren't listening. I'm just done."

I asked her a simple question: "What have you been saying all week?"

She thought for a moment and said, "Well… I've been saying just that. That I'm tired, frustrated, and done." I nodded. "That's the problem. You're prophesying your own stagnation."

Chapter 6: From Complaint to Confession

So we did something together. I gave her five scriptures to confess every day—morning and night. And I told her, "Even if you don't feel it, say it until you see it."

Thirty days later, she came back smiling. "I don't know how to explain it, Pastor. Things aren't perfect, but I feel different. I feel lighter. More confident."

Why? Because confession is construction.

Every word you speak is building either a prison or a platform. You get to choose.

I started practicing this personally. Every time I caught myself about to complain, I'd pause and flip it.

Instead of "I'm overwhelmed," I'd say, "I'm in demand because I'm gifted."

Instead of "This is too much," I'd say, "God, thank You for trusting me with this assignment."

Instead of "I can't catch a break," I'd say, "Goodness and mercy are following me."

PART 1: Change Your Thinking Change Your World

And the more I did it, the more my mindset shifted. Not because circumstances changed overnight—but because I stopped cursing what God was trying to bless.

Confession isn't magic. It's alignment.

It brings your mouth into agreement with God's mind.

And when your mind and your mouth line up with His Word—your life begins to follow.

So I challenge you: catch yourself this week. Monitor your words. Are you rehearsing the problem or declaring the promise? Are you venting or prophesying?

Write a confession list. Keep it near your mirror, your car, your phone. Speak it daily. Declare it boldly.

Because your words create your world.

It's time to shift. From complaint to confession. From murmuring to momentum. From stuck to soaring.

Let your mouth agree with the miracle God already prepared for you.

PART 1: Change Your Thinking Change Your World
And watch your life rise to meet the level of your confession.

Chapter 7: When the Enemy Is in Your Head

From the book: Change Your Mind, Change Your Life by Scott Gordon

---

Some of the hardest battles I've ever fought weren't in boardrooms, pulpits, or hospital rooms—they were in my own head.

You can be anointed and tormented. You can preach faith and wrestle with fear. You can lead others out of darkness while secretly trying to claw your way out of your own.

Nobody talks about that enough. But I will.

Because I know what it's like to be in a room full of people and still feel like you're not enough. I know what it's like to smile on the outside while your thoughts scream on the inside. I know what it's like to hear a voice that sounds like yours—but speaks against everything God says about you.

That's the enemy in your head.

The Bible is clear in 2 Corinthians 10:5—we must cast down imaginations and every high thing that exalts itself against the knowledge of God. That means there are *thoughts* that set themselves up as truth—even though they're lies. They challenge what God says and try to take the throne in your mind.

Thoughts like:

"You're a failure."

"You'll never change."

"God's done with you."

"Everyone sees through you."

If you don't confront those voices, they will build strongholds. Not demonic possession—but mental

Chapter 7: When the Enemy Is in Your Head

patterns. Fortresses of insecurity and shame that keep you from moving forward.

There was a season where I felt like I was going through the motions. Ministry on autopilot. I was doing everything right on the outside—but mentally, I was drained. Doubt was louder than destiny. Shame whispered constantly about past mistakes. And I couldn't shake the feeling that maybe I had missed my moment.

One night, I sat alone in my home office and just broke down. I said, "God, why am I thinking like this?"

And He answered me with one question: "Who told you that?"

Just like He asked Adam in the garden: "Who told you you were naked?" In other words, "Who gave you that idea? That identity? That insecurity? Because it didn't come from Me."

That question wrecked me. Because I realized—I had been agreeing with thoughts that didn't come from

PART 1: Change Your Thinking Change Your World

God. Thoughts formed in trauma, shaped by pressure, reinforced by silence.

It wasn't the devil shouting. It was me whispering lies I never healed from.

And that's when I understood: this isn't just spiritual warfare. It's *thought* warfare.

And your mind is the battlefield.

You don't win this war by ignoring the thoughts. You win by replacing them. You pull down every lie with truth. You take every thought captive. You tell it, "You don't belong here."

I started writing down the thoughts that came against me. I didn't just rebuke them—I replaced them.

The thought said, "You're broken." I said, "I'm fearfully and wonderfully made."

The thought said, "You'll lose everything." I said, "The Lord is my Shepherd, I shall not want."

Chapter 7: When the Enemy Is in Your Head

The thought said, "You don't have what it takes." I said, "Greater is He that is in me…"

This isn't cute Christian talk. This is war. And you don't win war with silence.

You've got to speak up. Out loud. With the Word.

When Jesus was tempted, He responded audibly. He didn't think scripture—He declared it.

That's what we must do. Every day. Not just in crisis, but as a lifestyle. Because the enemy doesn't take days off—and neither can your faith.

You've got to build a stronghold of truth.

How? By feeding on the Word. By surrounding yourself with people who speak life. By being honest when your mind is under attack. By getting help when the battle gets too heavy.

There's no shame in struggling. But there is danger in staying silent.

PART 1: Change Your Thinking Change Your World

You are not crazy. You are not weak. You are not disqualified.

You are in a fight. And it's one you can win.

But it starts with refusing to let the enemy build a house in your head.

Evict every lie. Cast down every imagination. And let the truth of God's Word take residence instead.

You are chosen. You are called. You are equipped.

You are enough.

Even when the enemy is in your head—God is in your heart. And His voice is stronger.

Tune in. Speak up. And take back your mind.

Chapter 8: The Daily Discipline of Renewal

From the book: Change Your Mind, Change Your Life by Scott Gordon

---

We love miracles, but we don't always love maintenance.

We want God to change our lives in one dramatic moment. And sometimes He does. But most of the time, transformation isn't an event—it's a discipline.

You don't become renewed because you shouted in service. You become renewed because you made a decision on Monday to keep thinking like the Word told you to on Sunday.

Romans 12:2 says, "Be transformed by the renewing of your mind." That's not past tense—it's present continuous. Which means it's not something you did once—it's something you keep doing. Day after day. Moment by moment.

Renewal is a lifestyle.

Years ago, I was talking to a young man who had given his life to Christ and was trying to change his ways. But he kept falling back into old patterns. He came to me frustrated: "Pastor, I don't think this is working. I'm praying. I'm trying. But nothing's changing."

I asked him one question: "What's your daily routine?"

He paused. "Well… I pray when I can. I read the Bible sometimes."

That was the issue.

You can't expect permanent change from occasional habits.

Renewal requires rhythm. It's not just about resisting old thoughts—it's about replacing them over and over until the new way of thinking becomes natural.

Chapter 8: The Daily Discipline of Renewal

When I was in one of the hardest seasons of my life, I had to go back to the basics. Not just preaching or attending church. I'm talking about waking up early to read a single scripture—and letting that one verse shape my entire day.

Sometimes it was five minutes. Sometimes it was an hour. But I learned this: it's not the length of time, it's the *consistency* that creates transformation.

We renew our minds the same way we train our bodies—through discipline.

The Apostle Paul said in 1 Corinthians 9:27, "I discipline my body and bring it into subjection…" In other words, this doesn't come easy. You have to *train* yourself to think differently.

Here's what my daily renewal started to look like:

1. **Wake up with worship** – Before scrolling my phone or checking messages, I'd whisper a thank-you to God. Set the tone with gratitude.
2. **Speak the Word aloud** – I had a list of

scriptures and confessions. Even if I didn't feel it, I said it.

3. **Feed my spirit before feeding my schedule** – Whether it was one verse or a devotional, I made sure God's voice came before the world's.

4. **Catch and correct thoughts throughout the day** – Every time I noticed a negative or fearful thought, I paused and replaced it with truth.

It wasn't about being perfect. It was about being *present* in the process.

And the more I did it, the more my mind began to shift. Not because life got easier—but because my mindset got stronger.

This is what many people miss. They want freedom, but they don't want structure. They want breakthrough, but not daily surrender.

Let me say this clearly: discipline is not legalism. It's faith in motion.

Chapter 8: The Daily Discipline of Renewal

It's saying, "God, I believe You so much that I'm going to build my day around Your Word, not just my feelings."

I've seen the difference it makes. In my own life. In others.

There's a woman in our church who struggled for years with depression and low self-worth. She'd come to every altar call, cry, shout, and go right back to her emotional prison.

Then one day she decided to go beyond the altar. She built a routine. Morning prayer. Daily confessions. Limiting negative input. Listening to worship instead of gossip. Reading a devotional with her kids at night.

Six months later, she was testifying with a new glow. "I didn't even realize when it shifted. But my thoughts aren't attacking me like they used to. I've got peace now."

That's what discipline will do. Quiet the chaos. Build your confidence. Create the space for the Holy Spirit to work.

PART 1: Change Your Thinking Change Your World

Because mind renewal isn't about hype—it's about habits.

You can't fight lifelong patterns with weekend faith. You need a daily encounter. A spiritual rhythm. A renewed routine.

I want to challenge you today: What does your daily mental diet look like? What are you feeding your mind before the world gets a hold of it?

Build your rhythm. Protect your mornings. Journal your thoughts. Declare the Word. Watch sermons. Write down victories.

You won't always feel the change right away. But one day, you'll look up and realize—you're not thinking like you used to. You're not reacting like you used to. You're walking different. Because you renewed your mind day by day.

Transformation isn't in the hype. It's in the habit.

Choose the rhythm. Embrace the discipline. And watch your whole life begin to change.

Chapter 9: Seeing Yourself the Way God Sees You

From the book: Change Your Mind, Change Your Life by Scott Gordon

---

You can't live differently until you think differently. And you can't think differently until you see yourself the way God sees you.

This is where so many people get stuck—not because they don't believe in God, but because they don't believe in who they are in God.

I've watched people sit in church for years, sing about victory, shout over breakthroughs, and still live in quiet defeat. Not because they don't love Jesus. But because they still carry a broken mirror.

They're trying to live for God while looking at themselves through the lens of rejection, abandonment, comparison, or failure.

I know the feeling.

There were times in my life where I could preach faith with power and still question if I was worthy of the platform I stood on. Where I could build houses, feed families, mentor young men—and still wrestle with a deep, unspoken sense of "not enough."

It wasn't about arrogance or false humility. It was about identity. Somewhere along the way, I had picked up the wrong image. And I had to learn how to replace it with what God said.

Ephesians 2:10 became a lifeline: "For we are God's masterpiece, created in Christ Jesus to do good works, which God prepared in advance for us to do."

Masterpiece. Not mistake. Not misfit. Not second-rate.

Chapter 9: Seeing Yourself the Way God Sees You

You are God's intentional, handcrafted design. And yet, so many of us see ourselves as broken pieces instead of God's masterpiece.

Why? Because we've let the wrong voices shape our vision.

Maybe it was something your parent said—or didn't say. Maybe it was the person who walked away. Maybe it was a church leader who wounded you. Maybe it was years of comparing yourself to others, wishing you had their story.

All of that forms a picture. And if you're not careful, that picture becomes your truth.

But it's not God's truth.

God doesn't define you by your past, your pain, or your performance. He defines you by His purpose.

You're not what happened to you. You're not what they called you. You're not the worst thing you've ever done.

PART 1: Change Your Thinking Change Your World

You are who God says you are.

The real breakthrough in renewing your mind is not just changing what you think—it's changing how you *see.*

I remember counseling a young woman who had come out of a toxic relationship. She was trying to rebuild her life but couldn't get past the feeling that she was "damaged goods."

She said, "Pastor, I know God forgives me. I just don't know how to forgive myself."

I looked her in the eye and said, "What if the issue isn't forgiveness—it's vision? What if you're still seeing yourself through the eyes of the one who broke you, instead of the One who made you?"

She cried. Because she knew it was true.

That conversation unlocked something—for her and for me.

Chapter 9: Seeing Yourself the Way God Sees You

How many of us are walking with blurred vision, living beneath our potential, simply because we haven't updated our identity to match God's truth?

When you start seeing yourself the way God does, everything shifts.

You start praying with boldness, not begging.

You start expecting favor instead of waiting for failure.

You stop shrinking to fit in rooms you were called to lead in.

This is not about ego. It's about agreement.

You either agree with the voice of fear, shame, and insecurity—or you agree with heaven.

And let me tell you something: heaven is not confused about who you are.

God sees a warrior when you see weakness.

He sees purpose when you see pain.

He sees royalty when you feel rejected.

But you've got to make the shift.

Start by writing down everything you've believed about yourself that doesn't line up with God's Word. Then, beside each one, write a scripture that tells the truth.

"I'm not good enough." → "I am the righteousness of God in Christ."

"I'm always overlooked." → "I am chosen, a royal priesthood, a holy nation."

"I can't recover from this." → "He restores my soul."

Speak these truths out loud every day. Put them on your mirror. Say them until you believe them.

Because as long as your self-image is broken, your faith walk will be too.

You were never meant to live from a place of lack. You were created to walk in love, confidence, and clarity.

Chapter 9: Seeing Yourself the Way God Sees You

See yourself the way heaven sees you. Stand in that identity. And watch your mind—and your life—completely transform.

Chapter 10: Think Like a Victor, Not a Victim

From the book: Change Your Mind, Change Your Life by Scott Gordon

---

One of the greatest shifts that will change your life is learning to think like a victor—even when life has tried to make you a victim.

Let me be clear. I'm not dismissing pain. I've sat with people in deep grief, trauma, betrayal, and abuse. I've walked through some dark valleys myself. There are real wounds. Real wrongs. Real reasons to feel broken.

But staying there is a choice.

You can acknowledge what happened without surrendering your power to it. You can heal from what broke you without letting it define you.

PART 1: Change Your Thinking Change Your World

Romans 8:37 says, "In all these things we are more than conquerors through him who loved us." It doesn't say we are victims. It doesn't say we are defeated. It says we're *more than conquerors*—in *all* these things.

That means no matter what comes against you, you have victory in your DNA. But you'll never walk in it until you start thinking like it.

The victim mindset says, "Life is happening to me." The victor mindset says, "God is working through me."

Victim thinking is passive. It waits to be rescued. It blames, complains, and stays stuck. Victor thinking is active. It prays, presses forward, and takes ownership of change.

I remember counseling a man who was constantly pointing to everything that went wrong in his life—his upbringing, his ex, his boss, even God. One day I said, "You've spent years rehearsing what they did. But when will you start taking responsibility for what you can do now?"

Chapter 10: Think Like a Victor, Not a Victim

He didn't like it at first. But a few months later, he came back and said it was the wake-up call he needed.

Sometimes we don't need more encouragement. We need a mindset adjustment.

Because you can't walk in power while living in pity.

Victim thinking is tricky because it often feels justified. "They really did hurt me." "I really was abandoned." "I never got the help I needed." And you're not wrong. But the danger is that pain becomes your home—and eventually your identity.

That's what happened to the man at the pool of Bethesda in John 5. He'd been sick for 38 years. Jesus walks up and asks him, "Do you want to be made whole?" And instead of answering yes, the man starts explaining why he can't get healed.

"No one helps me. Someone always gets in before me. I have no one."

PART 1: Change Your Thinking Change Your World

Jesus didn't ask about all that. He asked if the man *wanted* to be healed.

Because sometimes we get so attached to our story that we forget we can rise above it.

Jesus told him, "Rise, take up your bed, and walk."

No pity party. No long counseling session. Just a command to get up and shift his perspective.

That's the power of a victor's mindset.

I had to learn this myself. There was a time where I felt abandoned by people I had served faithfully. Lied on. Taken advantage of. I could have built a house in that pain. I could've justified closing off my heart and shrinking my calling.

But I remembered—victims stay down. Victors get up.

So I got up. Not because it was easy. But because the promise was too big to miss by staying bitter.

Chapter 10: Think Like a Victor, Not a Victim

The shift happened when I stopped asking "Why me?" and started saying "What now?"

Victors ask what now. They don't dwell in the past—they build in the present. They don't wait for life to be fair—they walk by faith anyway.

That's what Joseph did. His brothers betrayed him. Potiphar's wife lied on him. He was forgotten in prison. But nowhere in Scripture do you see Joseph with a victim attitude.

He kept rising. Kept working. Kept trusting.

And in the end, he looked at the very people who hurt him and said, "You meant it for evil, but God meant it for good."

That's the voice of a victor.

So here's the question I want you to wrestle with: Are you rehearsing your victim story or declaring your victory story?

PART 1: Change Your Thinking Change Your World

It's time to stop saying, "I always lose," and start saying, "I'm learning how to win."

Stop saying, "Nobody helps me," and start saying, "God is my helper."

Stop saying, "They ruined my life," and start saying, "God is restoring everything I lost."

Your words matter. Your posture matters. Your mindset matters.

Victors walk in rooms like they belong. They pray like God is listening. They plan like it's already done. They live like they're loved—because they are.

You are not a victim. You are not a mistake. You are not what they did to you.

You are a child of God. A conqueror. A world-changer.

It's time to think like it.

Drop the labels. Shake off the shame. Let go of the excuses. And rise.

Chapter 10: Think Like a Victor, Not a Victim

Think like a victor. Speak like a victor. Live like a victor.

Because that's exactly who you are.

Chapter 11: Teaching Others to Think Differently

From the book: Change Your Mind, Change Your Life by Scott Gordon

---

The proof that your mind is truly renewed isn't just how you live—it's how you lead.

God doesn't just want to transform you for you. He wants to use your transformation to change others.

2 Timothy 2:2 says, "And the things you have heard from me among many witnesses, commit these to faithful men who will be able to teach others also." That's legacy. That's discipleship. That's what happens when renewed minds multiply.

PART 1: Change Your Thinking Change Your World

I've always believed that changed people change people. And I've seen it. Not just in the pulpit, but in prison visits, at family reunions, in one-on-one conversations, and in quiet discipleship moments no one else saw.

When your mind shifts, your life becomes a mirror. Others begin to catch it, not just by what you say, but by how you carry yourself.

I'll never forget one young man who came up to me after a message I preached. I didn't lay hands on him. I didn't even know his story. But he looked me in the eyes and said, "Pastor, just watching you helped me believe I could become more."

That moment stuck with me. Because people are watching. Not to criticize—but to learn what's possible.

When you live with a renewed mind, you carry an atmosphere of possibility. You model freedom. And people who are still trapped start asking questions like, "How did you break out of that?" "How did you forgive them?" "How did you believe again after all you went through?"

Chapter 11: Teaching Others to Think Differently

That's your open door to teach.

Teaching doesn't always look like a Bible study. Sometimes it's a story. A testimony. A "this is what worked for me" moment. Sometimes it's walking with someone through their mess without judgment. Sometimes it's calling out the lie you hear in their voice and gently replacing it with truth.

I've sat with grown men—hard men—who broke down crying because no one ever told them they were allowed to think differently. To dream. To be free.

I've counseled women who were stuck in toxic cycles because everyone around them thought the same way—until they met someone who had been through it and made it out.

That's why you have to live this. Because your example will become someone's blueprint.

Don't hide your journey. Don't shrink from the change God has done in you. Let your mind be a testimony.

PART 1: Change Your Thinking Change Your World

Here's how you teach others to think differently:

1. **Live it consistently.** People don't need perfect. They need real. When they see your steady peace, your grounded faith, your joyful resilience—they'll want to know your secret.
2. **Speak life on purpose.** The way you talk becomes an education for others. Your words set the tone. Stop rehearsing what's wrong and start declaring what's possible.
3. **Call out the lie.** When someone says, "I'll never make it," don't just comfort—correct. "No, that's not true. You're more than a conqueror." Truth spoken in love is powerful.
4. **Share your story.** Tell people how your mind used to work. Let them know where you were and what helped you shift. People need to know you didn't always think this way.
5. **Create safe spaces for growth.** Whether in a church, a small group, your home, or over coffee—make room for people to talk, wrestle, and learn. Transformation thrives in trust.

Chapter 11: Teaching Others to Think Differently

You don't need a platform to be a teacher. You just need a renewed mind and a willing heart.

If you're a parent, your children are watching how you respond to stress, speak over your life, and handle disappointment. That's teaching.

If you're a leader, your team is learning from how you make decisions, how you treat people, and how you handle pressure. That's teaching.

If you're a friend, your mindset influences how others process pain and pursue healing. That's teaching.

We are all teachers. The question is: what are we teaching?

I've had to be intentional about this. I've learned to pause before I speak. To ask myself, "Is this the kind of thinking I want reproduced?" Because someone's listening. Always.

You may be the only renewed mind someone sees all week. Make it count.

PART 1: Change Your Thinking Change Your World

The goal isn't to impress people. It's to free them. One thought at a time.

Because once you've been pulled out of darkness, you've got a responsibility—and a privilege—to go back and get others.

You've seen the light. Now become it.

Teach others to think higher. To believe deeper.

To live freer.

Not just with sermons, but with your story.

Let your renewed mind be a classroom. Let your life be the syllabus. Let your breakthrough become someone else's invitation.

Because you didn't just change your mind for yourself. You changed it for everyone God's about to send your way.

Microphone and a stage. Sometimes it looks like a lunch meeting, a text message, a ride in the car. It's in those

Chapter 11: Teaching Others to Think Differently

everyday moments that your renewed mindset can unlock someone else's breakthrough.

But first, you have to be intentional.

You can't just live changed—you have to live *available*. Ask God: "Who am I called to pour into?" Then pay attention. The next conversation could be an assignment.

I've made it a habit to look for minds, not just behavior. When someone comes to me stuck, I don't just address what they're doing—I ask, "What are you thinking?" Because if you can locate the lie they're believing, you can start leading them out of it.

I've done this with young men who were caught in cycles of violence and poverty. With women battling shame. With leaders who lost their way. Every time, it started with helping them think differently.

Here's what I've learned: You can't change someone's life for them. But you *can* hand them the tools to build their own.

PART 1: Change Your Thinking Change Your World

You teach others to renew their minds by modeling truth, walking in love, and speaking life.

Modeling truth means being consistent. You can't preach faith and live in fear. You can't declare freedom and live in bitterness. A renewed mind walks what it talks.

Walking in love means being patient. People don't change overnight. Some folks will test your grace, question your motives, and even reject your help. But keep loving. The seed you plant today may not grow until next year—but it *will* grow.

Speaking life means using your words to create windows. When someone's stuck in darkness, your voice can be a window to light. Tell them who they are. Speak to their potential. Call out what they can't see in themselves.

When you speak life to a weary mind, you give it permission to believe again.

One of the greatest joys in my ministry has been watching people I once counseled now leading others. I've seen victims become mentors. I've seen men who once gave up now raising strong families. I've seen women who battled depression now walking in purpose and power.

That's what happens when you teach people to think differently.

Renewed minds reproduce.

If God has brought you out of something—He wants to use you to bring someone else out too.

You don't have to be perfect. You just have to be present. Willing. Obedient. Real.

Because somebody's freedom is connected to your testimony.

So don't keep your renewed mind to yourself.

Pour into your children. Speak over your spouse. Mentor that coworker. Start the Bible study. Host the prayer call. Write the book. Lead the small group. Share the story.

Whatever God has given you, give it away.

PART 1: Change Your Thinking Change Your World

Because when your mind is changed, your mission is clear.

You're not just called to be free. You're called to lead others to freedom.

Teach others to think differently. And watch God multiply everything He's done in you.

Chapter 12: Change Your Mind, Change Generations

From the book: Change Your Mind, Change Your Life by Scott Gordon

---

When you change your mind, you don't just change your mood, your money, or your momentum—you change your legacy.

This isn't just about breaking your own cycles. It's about breaking the cycles that have traveled through your bloodline for generations. It's about planting new patterns in your children, your grandchildren, and everyone who will come behind you.

Deuteronomy 30:19 says, "I have set before you life and death, blessings and curses. Now choose life, so that you and your descendants may live."

Did you catch that? Your choice—your mindset—doesn't just affect you. It affects your descendants.

When I began renewing my mind, I didn't realize I was rewriting my family's future. I just wanted to be free. I wanted peace. I wanted to think differently. But over time, I saw that my decisions were laying a foundation for my children to build on.

They didn't have to grow up in chaos like I did. They didn't have to learn survival the way I did. They were seeing stability. Faith. Love. Wisdom. Why? Because my mind got renewed.

You might be the first one in your family to break the poverty mindset. To reject bitterness. To walk in forgiveness. To tithe consistently. To own property. To believe God for more than just enough.

That's not just a victory. That's a new lineage.

People often talk about generational curses. But I believe just as strongly in generational *blessings.*

Chapter 12: Change Your Mind, Change Generations

When you start thinking differently, you start speaking differently. When you speak differently, your children hear differently. And when they hear differently, they believe differently.

This is legacy.

I remember one night sitting down with my son and daughter and asking, "What do you believe God is calling you to?" I listened as they shared dreams, goals, and convictions. And in that moment, I realized: they're not just dreaming because of what they see in the world—they're dreaming because of what they've seen in me.

Your mindset becomes someone else's permission slip.

When you walk in peace, your children learn peace is possible. When you walk in purpose, they learn they don't have to settle. When you handle storms with faith, they learn how to stand instead of sink.

That's why your renewed mind matters.

PART 1: Change Your Thinking Change Your World

Because you can leave your children money, but if you don't leave them a mindset, they'll lose what you gave them.

I've seen it too many times—inheritance without identity. Wealth without wisdom. Gifts without grounding.

But not in my house.

I decided a long time ago: the curse stops with me. The trauma stops with me. The fear, the doubt, the spiritual laziness—stops with me.

My children will see faith. My grandchildren will know prayer. My great-grandchildren will inherit legacy.

Not because I'm perfect. But because I made a decision to renew my mind and build a new pattern.

That's what I want for you.

Don't just think for yourself. Think for those coming behind you.

Chapter 12: Change Your Mind, Change Generations

What kind of language do you want spoken in your home? What kind of faith do you want modeled? What kind of peace do you want normalized?

It all starts with your mindset.

It starts with you choosing truth over trauma. Vision over victimhood. Victory over survival.

You may be the first one to step out. To believe big. To go back to school. To get counseling. To start the business. To build a healthy marriage. To say, "We don't do that anymore."

And you may feel alone. But you're not. You're setting a new standard.

You're the generational curse breaker. The stronghold smasher. The mindset renovator.

You're not just changing your mind—you're changing your *bloodline.*

So stand tall. Speak life. Pray hard. Live with purpose.

PART 1: Change Your Thinking Change Your World

And know this: every thought you bring into alignment with God's Word is building a foundation that your family will stand on for generations.

You're not just a person with a renewed mind.

You're a patriarch. A matriarch. A pioneer.

You are the start of a new story.

So go forward. Break the cycle. Change the pattern. Set the example.

Because when you change your mind—you change generations.

PART: 2
Who Is Scott L. Gordon?

A Journey of Faith, Favor, and Fortitude

by Scott L. Gordon

Chapter 1: Early Life and Upbringing

Theme: Formation Through Fire

Before the titles, before the real estate, before the pulpits and the buildings, there was a boy—a quiet observer of chaos, a survivor of disruption.

Scott L. Gordon was born into a world that didn't wait for him to find his footing. He was placed into the arms of his grandparents in Sapulpa Oklahoma, where life was humble but steady. There was love there, the kind that didn't need to be spoken every day because it was shown in work, in food on the table, and in consistency. His grandfather worked at the brickyard across the tracks, his clothes stained in the red clay of labor, but his heart full of quiet strength. His grandmother was the keeper of the home—strict but faithful, a woman who didn't have much but made what she had stretch.

That small window of stability didn't last forever. One day, without warning, Scott was uprooted. His aunt came to take him, and he left everything he knew behind. No one asked him what he wanted. There was no suitcase packed with care—just a shift, sudden and sharp. He was taken to a different side of life, placed into a four-bedroom house packed with children, noise, and survival. Six of his aunt's children, three of his mother's sons, and a few others all shared the same air. It was a house full of people but hollow with confusion. There was no room for questions, no explanations.

Just the expectation that you adapt.

Scott was a boy learning early what many men never do—how to survive displacement without letting it define you. The home was crowded, the love was scarce, and the rules were ever-changing. But he began to find his place, not through comfort, but through contribution. He learned to work. If something needed to be done, you did it. If there was a way to earn, you found it. That's when the seeds of grit were planted.

By sixth grade, Scott had his first job. He cleaned yards, pulled weeds, and pushed lawnmowers across town. He didn't wait to be told—he looked for needs and met them. His hands grew calloused, and so did his spirit. Not bitter, just determined. That determination grew as he watched others around him give in to the pressure, while he kept pressing forward.

Even in the midst of this chaos, there were glimmers of purpose. Church on Sunday was non-negotiable. The preaching, the music, the structure—it was a contrast to the unpredictability of home. He sat in pews, half-listening and half-dreaming. Something about those services—about the God people spoke of—planted hope in him. A whisper that said,

"There's more."

The early years of Scott L. Gordon's life weren't marked by luxury or affirmation. They were marked by motion, by migration, by the constant tension between staying invisible and staying alive. And yet, those very years built in him the muscle of resolve. The ability to get up, even when knocked down. The vision to see past what was, into what could be.

He didn't know it then, but the pain was preparing him. The instability was shaping him. And the God he barely understood was already walking
beside him.

These were the years that formed him through fire. And he would never be the same.

Chapter 2:
The Making of a Man

Theme: Grit, Grind, and Grace

Manhood didn't arrive with a speech, a celebration, or a father handing down wisdom. It came to Scott L. Gordon through grit, grind, and grace.

There were no shortcuts—only the pressure of life forcing a boy to grow up faster than he should have. And Scott? He answered that pressure
with persistence.

By the time most kids were thinking about cartoons and birthday parties, Scott was thinking about money—how to make it, how to stretch it,
and how not to be a burden on anyone. His first job came in the sixth grade. He cleaned, mowed, raked, and ran errands. Every dollar he made was earned by sweat. Every dime felt like freedom.

Chapter 2: The Making of a Man

His mind didn't operate like the average kid's. He wasn't thinking about allowance—he was thinking about legacy. Not the kind you inherit, but the kind you build. That drive came from watching the women in his life struggle to feed the house. It came from watching older boys lose themselves in fast money and dead-end streets. Scott didn't want to be next—he wanted to be different.

By ninth grade, he was running small businesses. Breaking horses. Raising rabbits. Selling candy. He didn't need a mentor to tell him how to hustle—life taught him. He bought cages, fed livestock, and figured out market demand. He'd raise rabbits and sell them buy candy take it to school after the bell rang. On the school bus, he sold candy like a vendor with a license. Supply and demand made sense to him before algebra ever did.

But behind the hustle was hurt. He never said it out loud, but he felt the gap—what it meant to not have a father around. What it meant to be the one others leaned on, even when he had nothing left to give. He learned to smile when he wanted to cry. He learned to press forward when his heart was broken. He learned to pretend he didn't care when he was really screaming on the inside.

He also began to understand something else: money could solve problems, but it couldn't heal pain. He could buy clothes, snacks, and moments
of respect—but he couldn't buy identity. That would have to come from somewhere deeper.

Even in the streets, Scott had a kind of light about him. Older guys noticed it. He didn't talk much, but when he did, people listened. They trusted him. His word mattered. And as the world tried to mold him into one thing, God was already shaping him into another. He didn't even know it yet—but God was setting him apart.

There were days Scott questioned whether he mattered. Whether life would ever be more than just survival. But somehow, he kept showing up.

To school. To work. To responsibility. He kept grinding when quitting would've been easier. And that choice—to stay in the race—is what quietly forged the man inside the boy.

Chapter 2: The Making of a Man

In those teenage years, Scott didn't just build income. He built endurance. He didn't just make money. He made a name for himself—a reputation of honor, work ethic, and reliability. And even though the world around him still felt unstable, he started to feel something solid within him.

That was the grace of God. Not loud. Not flashy. But present. It was grace that shielded him from the wrong crowd. Grace that redirected him when temptation came. Grace that whispered, "You're not like them." And grace that gave him the strength to keep becoming.

The making of a man doesn't come with applause. It comes with decisions. It comes with pain. It comes with perseverance. And for Scott L. Gordon, those years weren't easy—but they were necessary.

They didn't break him.

They built him.

Chapter 3:
The Call to Ministry

Theme: When Destiny Interrupts

The call of God rarely comes when you're ready. More often, it shows up when you're running. That was true for Scott L. Gordon.

He didn't grow up wanting to be a preacher. Ministry wasn't a childhood dream—it was a divine interruption. The streets were more familiar than the pulpit. Hustling came easier than holiness. And yet, there was always a whisper in his spirit—soft, but steady—that said, "You were made for more."

Scott tried to drown that voice in work, in money, in survival, and even in relationships. But the call wouldn't go away. Even when he wasn't listening, God was still speaking.

Chapter 3: The Call to Ministry

The shift didn't come all at once. It came in moments—moments where the crowd went quiet and conviction got loud. Moments where he have lost everything. Moments where he saw others fall and somehow knew he was being spared. Grace was working undercover, building an altar in a heart that still looked like a battlefield.

The first time Scott really acknowledged the call, it wasn't with a pulpit—it was with a prayer. A simple, broken, honest surrender. Not polished.

Not churchy. Just real. "God, if you'll still have me, I'll follow." And heaven heard it.

Doors began to open that he didn't knock on. Pastor Ruth saw something in him. affirmed him. But more importantly, he started to see himself
through God's eyes. Not as the boy from the crowded house. Not as the hustler. But as a man chosen—called—not because of perfection, but because
of purpose.

Scott started preaching. Raw, real, and full of fire. He didn't sound like anyone else because he wasn't trying to.

He spoke from lived experience.

From pain. From process. And people responded. Not because he had all the answers—but because he wasn't afraid to tell the truth.

Then came the divine assignment. In August 2001, the senior pastor of Calvary Baptist Church in Sapulpa passed away suddenly. The church was in shock. The people were grieving. They needed leadership. They needed direction. And somehow, all eyes turned to Scott.

He didn't feel qualified. He wasn't chasing the position. But the spirit of God made it clear—this wasn't about being ready. It was about being willing.

He was asked to serve as interim pastor. And what was supposed to be temporary became a permanent move of God. In February 2002, Scott L. Gordon was officially installed as the senior pastor of Calvary Baptist Church.

He didn't inherit a perfect church. But he brought something powerful to the pulpit: vision, authenticity, and the willingness to grow publicly.

He preached what he lived and lived what he preached. He didn't just call people to faith—he showed them what it looked like in motion.

Under his leadership, the church didn't just survive—it thrived. Ministries expanded. Souls were saved. Families were restored. And while the
building was important, the focus was never on the steeple—it was always on the people.

Scott never forgot where he came from. He never stopped being the young man who cleaned yards and sold rabbits. He just added a microphone. A
Bible. A mandate.

This chapter of his life wasn't about image—it was about impact.

And though he stepped into ministry unexpectedly, the truth is—he was called all along. Every pain, every hustle, every setback—it had all been preparation for the moment when destiny interrupted.

The call wasn't just to preach.

It was to lead.

To love.

To heal.

To shepherd.

And Scott L. Gordon said yes.

Chapter 4: Building While Broken

Theme: Leading Through Pain, Living Through Purpose

Most people want to lead from strength. But Scott L. Gordon learned how to lead from brokenness.

There's a unique weight that comes with being a pastor. People expect answers. They look for strength. They lean on you in crisis, ask you to pray when the storms hit, and expect you to be a well that never runs dry. But what happens when the one everyone leans on is bleeding inside?

Scott found out.

After becoming senior pastor of Calvary Baptist Church, he stepped into a leadership role that required more than sermons. It required heart.

Chapter 4: Building While Broken

It required stamina. And it required him to give, even when he was running on empty. Most people saw the growth—the packed pews, the community outreach, the ministries flourishing. What they didn't see was the weight he carried home.

He was counseling families while his own heart was cracking. He was leading prayer circles while asking God to hold his own world together. He was officiating weddings while grieving personal loss. It wasn't always visible, but it was real. There were days he stood behind the pulpit with tears that hadn't dried. Nights when he prayed for others and silently hoped someone was praying for him.

And yet—he kept showing up.

He didn't fake his faith. He fought for it. He didn't preach empty words. He preached through the storm. And somehow, God kept using him—not in spite of the pain, but through it.

At the same time, he was working full-time as a hospice chaplain. Every day, he entered homes where life was ending. He held hands of the dying.

He comforted grieving families. He offered peace in moments when words felt powerless. That kind of work changes you. It confronts you with the fragility of life—and the urgency of purpose.

While others were clocking out at five, Scott was often doing bedside ministry at night, preaching on Sundays, and managing real estate properties on the side. His schedule didn't leave much time for rest, but his calling wouldn't let him quit.

In those same years, God was birthing something new in him: vision for community transformation. He started buying homes—one at a time—believing that the same God who called him to pastor people could also call him to rebuild neighborhoods. It wasn't glamorous. He didn't have investor backing or a trust fund. Just favor. Just faith.

Chapter 4: Building While Broken

And with that faith, he started flipping houses, renting to families, restoring properties others had abandoned. His mission wasn't just to profit—it was to prove that revival could come to broken streets the same way it came to broken hearts.

But through it all—he was still hurting.
There were seasons when the loneliness crept in. Seasons when his marriage felt fragile. Seasons when betrayal hit close to home. He carried burdens he couldn't always talk about. Because when you're the leader, people assume you're invincible.

But Scott learned that healing doesn't disqualify you from helping. In fact, it qualifies you even more.
He began to speak more openly. Not recklessly, but honestly. He started writing books, sharing wisdom, and mentoring others—not from a platform of perfection, but from the trenches of process. He became a pastor that others could relate to—not because he had all the answers, but because he wasn't afraid to wrestle with the questions.

PART: 2 Who Is Scott L. Gordon?

Building while broken doesn't mean you're faking it. It means you've decided that pain won't stop your purpose

Scott L. Gordon built churches, businesses, and trust—while carrying a heart that was still healing. And every nail, every message, every property,
every hug was a declaration of faith.

That God still uses the broken.
That ministry is still worth it.
That you can hurt and still help.

He is a living reminder: just because you're broken doesn't mean you're done.

Chapter 5: Real Estate and Restoration

Theme: Faith That Buys Back the Block

Scott L. Gordon didn't get into real estate to get rich. He got into real estate to take back what was lost.

It started with one house. No roadmap. No inheritance. No real estate license. Just a sense that the same God who gave him a pulpit could also give him property. And not just to own—but to transform.

He walked into a neighborhood where others only saw decline. Overgrown lots. Abandoned homes. Hopeless families renting from landlords who never cared. But Scott saw something else—*promise*. He saw potential where others saw problems. He saw community where others saw collapse.

Chapter 5: Real Estate and Restoration

That's when it began.

He bought his first house through faith and hustle. He negotiated with sellers. He learned how to budget repairs, work with contractors, pull permits, and manage tenants—all while still preaching, visiting hospice patients, and leading a church.

He flipped that one house. Then another. Then ten. Then fifty.

Each house had a story. Some were drug houses. Some were burned-out shells. Others were just forgotten—left to rot on streets that used to be filled with children playing and families thriving. But Scott didn't just renovate buildings—he reclaimed territory. Every roof replaced, every floor repaired, every wall painted was an act of ministry. It was restoration, not just renovation

And he didn't stop.

Scott grew his portfolio to over 350 rooftops—single-family homes, duplexes, commercial buildings, even churches. He created lease-to-own opportunities for

PART: 2 Who Is Scott L. Gordon?

families who never thought they'd own anything. He gave people second chances—tenants with backgrounds, single mothers with kids, men trying to rebuild their lives.

He became not just a landlord, but a lifeline.

But it wasn't easy.

Contractors bailed. Pipes burst. Tenants skipped rent. And sometimes he had to fund payroll and repairs out of his own pocket. There were seasons when everything seemed to go wrong at once—houses vandalized, appliances stolen, roofs leaking. Yet through it all, he never lost sight of the mission.

Because for Scott, real estate wasn't about collecting properties. It was about restoring dignity.
He had a great partner who mentored him Melvin Matthews. He bought and remodeled churches that were boarded up. He turned empty buildings into community hubs. He employed people from neighborhoods others had given up on. And as his business grew, so did his

ability to impact lives—not just on Sunday, but every day of the week.

Scott began teaching others how to do the same. He mentored young investors. He spoke at conferences. He wrote books like "Property Wealth" and "Walking in the Overflow" to show that ownership isn't just for the elite—it's for the faithful. For those willing to believe God for more.

He coined the phrase: "Buy all the land you can." Not because of greed, but because of *legacy*. Because when you own the land, you influence what happens on it. And when the righteous own the land, communities change.

There's a scripture that says, "The earth is the Lord's and the fullness thereof." Scott believes that. But he also believes the Lord gives stewardship to those who walk in obedience, discipline, and vision.

And that's exactly what he's done.

PART: 2 Who Is Scott L. Gordon?

He's taken his story—from trauma to transformation—and planted it into streets, bricks, and deeds. And in doing so, he's proven that faith doesn't just speak. It builds. It renovates. It invests. It multiplies.

Scott L. Gordon is not just a real estate investor.

He's a restorer of the breach.
A repairer of homes and hearts.
A Kingdom builder in blueprints and concrete.

And it all started with one house… and one yes.

Chapter 6: Global Mission and Local Impact

Theme: From Tulsa to the Nations

Scott L. Gordon has never believed in small thinking. While his feet were planted in Sapulpa, Sand Springs and Tulsa, his heart always beat for the world.

What started in the streets and sanctuaries of Oklahoma soon stretched across borders and oceans. Scott didn't just want to preach to the people in his city—he wanted to touch nations. Not for fame. Not for photo ops. But because he believed deeply in the mandate of the Gospel: "Go into all the world."

His first international mission trip opened his eyes in a way that no classroom or seminary ever could. In Nicaragua, he saw hunger and hope living side by side. Children with no shoes still lifted their hands in worship.

Chapter 6: Global Mission and Local Impact

Families with barely enough to eat still shared their food with strangers. It broke him—and it built him.

From there, the journey expanded.

He served in Ghana, where the heat was relentless but the hunger for the Word of God was stronger. He walked through villages that didn't have clean water, yet still had vibrant worship. He helped build structures for worship, delivered supplies, and prayed for people who had never seen a man from Tulsa—but welcomed him like family.

In Kenya, he visited Nairobi and ministered in the slums—areas where children grew up with no electricity, no running water, and no education system. But what they lacked in infrastructure, they made up for in faith. Scott stood in tin-roof churches preaching hope to people who only had one pair of shoes—but had limitless joy.

He preached in the Dominican Republic, where language barriers didn't stop the Spirit from moving. And in London, he witnessed the spiritual hunger of a nation rich in history but struggling in faith. He brought his story to platforms that never expected it—but needed it.

Through each trip, he never went just to speak—he went to serve. He brought clothes. Built latrines. Sponsored children. Supplied Bibles. And more than anything, he brought the love of God in action. Hands that helped. Ears that listened. A presence that stayed long after the plane took off.

But Scott didn't forget his own backyard.
Back in Sapulpa and Tulsa, he started feeding programs with his church and ministry team. He partnered with community leaders to launch homeless outreach efforts. Every Thanksgiving, Christmas, and throughout the year, his team showed up with food, blankets, prayer, and compassion. They didn't wait for people to come to church—they *became* the church in the streets.

For over a decade, he supported and led an outreach team that fed the homeless and helped transition people into homes.

He didn't just give food—he gave dignity. Conversations. Opportunities. Prayer. He worked with returning citizens—men and women getting out of prison—giving them jobs, mentoring, and a second chance.

He also served on nonprofit boards and civic organizations, using his voice and influence to advocate for justice, housing, education, and economic equity. He worked alongside foundations, local schools, and business leaders to make tangible change.

Scott understood something most leaders overlook: if your Gospel doesn't reach the streets, it's incomplete.

So he made it his mission to go beyond Sunday morning. Beyond the building. Beyond the comfort zone.

He modeled a Kingdom that moves—across continents, through neighborhoods, into broken places with healing power.

To the world, he may be a pastor, a speaker, or a builder

But to the people he's touched—whether in Tulsa or Kenya—he's something much more:

A brother.

A servant.

A light in dark places.

And his global mission has always started with one question:

"How can I help?"

Chapter 7: Author, Teacher, Visionary

Theme: Writing to Heal, Teaching to Build

Long before Scott L. Gordon became a bestselling author, he was a storyteller—one who carried decades of experience, lessons, and pain in his spirit.

But it wasn't until God told him to start writing that he began to truly unpack what was inside.

Scott never set out to become an author for status or popularity. He started writing because the burden inside him wouldn't stay quiet. The wisdom he had gained—from childhood trauma, ministry challenges, business lessons, and personal battles—had to be shared. Not for applause, but for assignment.

Chapter 7: Author, Teacher, Visionary

His first books were more than words—they were tools. Messages of breakthrough, strategies of faith, and transparent stories that helped others walk out of darkness. Titles like *Property Wealth* showed people how to move from renting to owning, from poverty to legacy. It wasn't just real estate—it was a mindset shift. A new way of seeing land, stewardship, and economic empowerment.

In his teaching *The God-Kind of Faith*, he broke down what it means to believe beyond the natural. He didn't write it as a theologian—he wrote it as a man who had to believe when there was no money, no opportunity, and no help. That kind of faith—the kind that builds with no blueprint—is what birthed his business, sustained his ministry, and healed his soul.

Then came *Helping While Hurting*—a deeply personal look into the life of someone who has ministered to others while managing his own pain. In his life, Scott opened wounds that had never been seen publicly. He shared stories about childhood abandonment, broken relationships, and silent seasons of grief. And he did it to give others permission to heal while still being called.

His writing didn't stop at books. Scott taught workshops, created curriculum, led seminars, and developed training tools for pastors, entrepreneurs, and leaders across the country. His teachings were practical, but powerful. He didn't just quote scripture—he gave structure. He didn't just shout truth—he gave templates.

Whether it was teaching pastors how to lead with integrity, business owners how to scale with faith, or men how to rise with responsibility, Scott built a reputation as a voice of clarity, conviction, and compassion.

He also saw beyond the moment. Scott has always had vision—not just for what is, but for what could be. He would walk into a dilapidated house and see a beautiful rental. He would speak to a teenager in trouble and see a future leader. He would talk to a burned-out pastor and see fresh fire.

Chapter 7: Author, Teacher, Visionary

He's a Kingdom visionary—not confined to pulpits or properties. His gift is seeing potential. His call is activating it.

That's what makes him more than a teacher. He's a multiplier. A builder of builders. A writer of roads others can walk on.

And every book he's written… every lesson he's taught… every dream he's cast… is marked by one thing:

He wants you to win.

Not just spiritually—but in life.
Not just on Sunday—but every day.
Not just in prayer—but in purpose.

Scott L. Gordon is proof that what you survive can become what you teach.

And he's only getting started.

Chapter 8: The Man Behind the Mission

Theme: What the World Doesn't See

Behind the titles, the travels, the teachings, and the testimonies is a man—real, raw, and still becoming.

Scott L. Gordon may be a pastor, a builder, an author, and a businessman—but when the doors close, and the lights go down, he's still a man with a heart, with struggles, with joys and regrets. He has fought battles no one knew about. He has celebrated wins in silence and cried over losses no one saw coming.

That's what people often miss about leaders: they bleed too.

Scott has loved deeply. He has been a husband, a father, a brother, and a friend. He's made sacrifices few will

Chapter 8: The Man Behind the Mission

ever understand. There were times he gave when he didn't have it. Times he stayed when he wanted to run. Times he poured into others while trying to keep himself from drowning.

He's walked through storms that shook his faith—but never stole it.

There were seasons of silence where it felt like God was far. There were heartbreaks that left scars, not just on his life, but on his soul. He's wrestled with loneliness, leadership pressure, betrayal, and the weight of being strong for everyone else.

But through it all—he kept showing up.

Not perfect. Not untouched by life. But still willing. Still available. Still believing.

He's the kind of man who will show up for a stranger's funeral, then go back to fix a rental house, then sit at a board meeting, then write a book at midnight. He's lived a hundred lives in one—and yet still shows up like he's just getting started.

Scott doesn't talk much about his pain, unless it helps someone else heal. He doesn't flaunt his accomplishments, but he does share his process—because he knows someone's breakthrough might be hiding in his story.

He's a man who wrestles with God—not because he doubts Him, but because he wants more of Him. A man who still prays for his children in secret. A man who still apologizes when he misses the mark. A man who still asks God to search his heart.

Scott isn't impressed by applause. He's moved by impact. He's not chasing followers. He's chasing legacy. He's not trying to go viral. He's trying to be
faithful.

And while the world may celebrate his accomplishments, the real victory is in what most people never see:

- The quiet prayers.
- The lonely drives.
- The nights he almost gave up.
- The mornings he got up anyway.

Chapter 8: The Man Behind the Mission

The man behind the mission is not a superhero. He's not flawless. He's not unshakable.

But he is faithful.

And in the end, that's what matters most.

Because God doesn't call the flawless. He calls the faithful.

And Scott L. Gordon is still showing up.

Still serving.

Still healing.

Still building.

Still becoming.

Conclusion

Theme: Still Becoming

So who is Scott L. Gordon?

He is more than a pastor. More than an investor. More than a leader. He is living proof that God can take the broken pieces of a man's story and turn them into a mosaic of purpose.

He is a builder—not just of homes, but of people. Of dreams. Of movements. He is a restorer—not just of properties, but of hope. Of communities. Of faith.

He is a fighter—not just in business or ministry—but in spirit. One who has warred in prayer, warred in private, and still kept his head up through every storm.

His life is not a highlight reel. It is a journey. One marked by detours and delays, but also divine acceleration. A story where pain has purpose, and process has power.

Conclusion

Every chapter—from childhood to calling, from business to burden—reveals a deeper truth: **God's favor has been the thread all along.**

He is the founder of a legacy that will outlive him. The father of a future that he fought to create. The voice of a generation of men and women who need to see that yes—God still uses the overlooked, the underestimated, the underfunded, and the unqualified.

He is not done. The chapters are still unfolding. The vision is still expanding. The assignment is still active.

And if you asked him what matters most, he wouldn't talk about houses, or pulpits, or books.

He would probably say something like this:

"I'm just grateful God still uses me. That He didn't give up on me. That He called me… and I said yes."

That's who Scott L. Gordon is.

And by God's grace… he's still becoming.

PART: 2 Who Is Scott L. Gordon?

Who Is Scott L. Gordon?

A Journey of Faith, Favor, and Fortitude

What happens when a boy raised in pain becomes a man called by purpose?

From a crowded house into international pulpits, from cleaning yards to owning entire blocks, Scott L. Gordon's life is a testimony of grace, grit, and God's unshakable favor. In this deeply personal memoir, Scott opens the vault of his journey—unfiltered and unforgettable.

He shares how he survived abandonment, built a multimillion-dollar real estate portfolio, pastored through heartbreak, and preached across nations—all while learning to trust a God who never let go.

Each chapter reveals another layer of the man behind the mission: the pastor who led while bleeding, the builder who saw beauty in boarded-up homes, the servant who turned pain into power.

Whether you're a leader, a dreamer, or someone just trying to hold it together—this book will meet you where you are and push you to believe again.

Because when God's hand is on your life, nothing you've been through is wasted.

Final Charge

You've read the chapters. You've seen what's possible. Now it's your turn. Don't stop at inspiration—move into transformation. Your new life starts with a new mindset. Every page you just read was a seed. Water it with faith. Declare it over your life. And remember—you don't just have the power to change. You have the power to lead others into change too. Go live the renewed life. And never forget—when you change your mind, you change your life.